W9-CNE-907

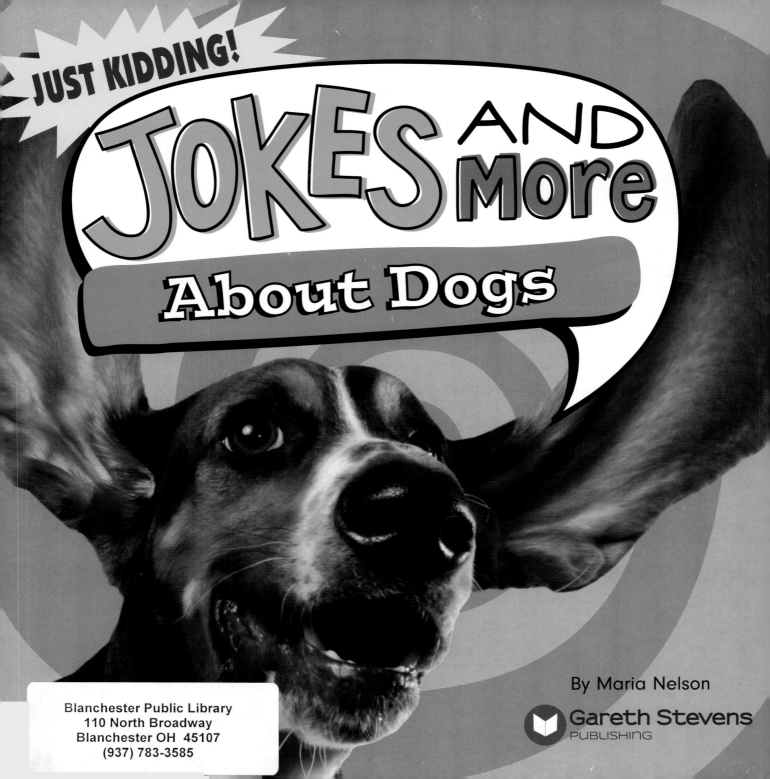

JUST KIDDING!

JOKES AND More

About Dogs

By Maria Nelson

Gareth Stevens
PUBLISHING

Please visit our website, www.garethstevens.com. For a free color catalog of all our high-quality books, call toll free 1-800-542-2595 or fax 1-877-542-2596.

Library of Congress Cataloging-in-Publication Data

Nelson, Maria.
Jokes and more about dogs / by Maria Nelson.
    p. cm. — (Just kidding!)
Includes index.
ISBN 978-1-4824-0542-2 (pbk.)
ISBN 978-1-4824-0545-3 (6-pack)
ISBN 978-1-4824-0543-9 (library binding)
1. Wit and humor, Juvenile. 2. Dogs — Miscellanea — Juvenile literature. I. Nelson, Maria. II. Title.
PN6163.N45 2014
818—dc23
First Edition

Published in 2015 by
Gareth Stevens Publishing
111 East 14th Street, Suite 349
New York, NY 10003

Designer: Sarah Liddell
Editor: Kristen Rajczak

Photo credits: Cover, pp. 1, 7, 22 (basset hound) Annette Shaff/Shutterstock.com; pp. 5, 20 WilleeCole/Shutterstock.com; pp. 6, 9, 10, 13, 14, 17, 18 Igor Zakowski/Shutterstock.com; p. 8 Fuse/Getty Images; p. 11 Mat Hayward/Shutterstock.com; p. 12 Javier Brosch/Shutterstock.com; p. 15 Linn Currie/Shutterstock.com; p. 16 danilobiancalana/Shutterstock.com; p. 19 Eponaleah/Shutterstock.com; p. 21 aerogondo2/Shutterstock.com; p. 22 (Pekingese) viki2win/Shutterstock.com.

Printed in the United States of America

CPSIA compliance information: Batch #CS15GS: For further information contact Gareth Stevens, New York, New York at 1-800-542-2595.

Contents

Words in the glossary appear in **bold** type the first time they are used in the text.

Wag Your Tail!

Dogs are more like people than you might think. They dream and even have taste buds. But some of their habits seem pretty funny! They chase their tails, race around in circles, and try to catch toads and bugs in their mouths.

Even sillier, some owners dress their dogs in costumes! Oddly enough, this isn't a new practice. During the **Middle Ages**, Great Danes and mastiffs wore suits of **armor**. Imagine how funny that would look today!

All About the Breed

When is a black dog not a black dog?
When it's a greyhound.

What kind of dog does a **vampire** have?

A bloodhound.

What kind of dog does a mad scientist have?
A **laboratory** retriever.

Silly Sayings

What did the Dalmatian say after dinner?

"That hit the spots!"

What did one hungry dog say to another?
"Let's get some chow chow."

What did the mother dog say to her children?

"Hush, puppies."

What did the tired dog say when he got home from work?
"I had a ruff day."

9

Name Play

What do you get when you cross a dog and a vegetable?

A collieflower.

What's a sick dog called?
A germy shepherd.

What's a dog's favorite pie topping?
Cool whippet.

10

Puppy Chow

What do dogs eat at the movies?

Pupcorn.

12

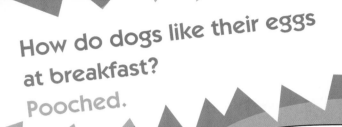

13

Lots to Do

What do lazy dogs do for fun?
Chase parked cars.

Why did the dog carry a clock?

He wanted to be a watchdog.

Where do you leave your dog when you go downtown?
The barking lot.

Inside, Outside

What happens when it rains cats and dogs?

You could step in a poodle!

Give the Dog a Bone

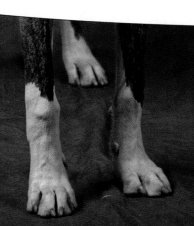

Begging for More

What did the cowboy say when his dog ran away?
Well, doggone!

What do dogs increase?
The pupulation.

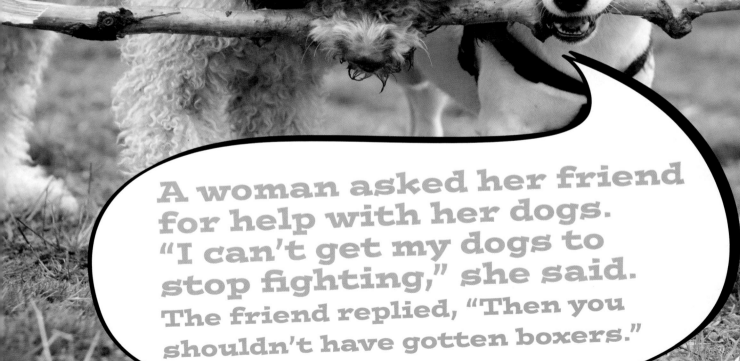

Why did the dog feel sad about being called a "good dog"?
It was a Great Dane.

A woman asked her friend for help with her dogs. "I can't get my dogs to stop fighting," she said. The friend replied, "Then you shouldn't have gotten boxers."

Fun and Funny Facts About Dogs

Dogs **pant** in order to keep cool. They might take 300 to 400 breaths in a minute!

Puppies are born blind. Their eyelids stay closed until their eyes are grown enough.

A dog's nose print is **unique**. Like a fingerprint, it can help **identify** the dog.

Dogs have a sense of smell 10,000 to 100,000 times more powerful than that of people.

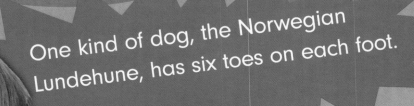

One kind of dog, the Norwegian Lundehune, has six toes on each foot.

22

Glossary

armor: a thick metal covering worn by soldiers in battle

breed: a group of animals that share features different from other groups of the kind

identify: to find out the name or features of something

laboratory: a place with tools to perform experiments

Middle Ages: a time in European history from about 500 to 1500

pant: to breathe quickly and heavily

unique: being the only one of its kind

vampire: a made-up being who drinks human blood

For More Information

BOOKS

Halls, Kelly Milner. *Courageous Canine: And More True Stories of Amazing Animal Heroes.* Washington, DC: National Geographic Society, 2013.

Niven, Felicia Lowenstein. *Hysterical Dog Jokes to Tickle Your Funny Bone.* Berkeley Heights, NJ: Enslow Publishers, Inc., 2014.

WEBSITES

Animal Jokes for Kids
www.activityvillage.co.uk/animal_jokes.htm
Find lots more jokes about all kinds of animals.

Dog Breed Selectors
animal.discovery.com/breed-selector/dog-breeds.html
Thinking about getting a dog? Use Animal Planet's website to help you pick out the perfect pup!